THE ULTIMATE LEADERSHIP WORKBOOK FOR CRISIS MANAGEMENT

Eric Jackier

© Eric Jackier 2020

Copyright © 2020 by Eric Jackier

All Rights Reserved

Cover and art design
By
Write My Wrongs Self-Publishing

No part of this book may be reproduced, stored in a retrieval system, or transmitted by any means, electronic, mechanical, photocopying, recording or otherwise without written permission from the author

www.jtdcoaching.com

The Ultimate Leadership Workbook for Crisis Management

Eric Jackier

ACKNOWLEDGEMENTS

This workbook is dedicated to our incredible medical professionals who serve as leaders and our frontline defense during the coronavirus pandemic.

Your work has been incredible and will never be forgotten.

Thank you for everything you are doing to keep us safe and healthy.

CONTENTS

About the Author	9
Introduction	11
Chapter 1: **Decide You Will Succeed No Matter What!**	11
Chapter 2: **Develop Your Leadership Routine**	13
Chapter 3: **Creating Your 90-Day Plan**	16
Chapter 4: **Communicate Often and Effectively**	18
Chapter 5: **Building Your Crisis Management Team**	21
Chapter 6: **Talk to Your Creditors**	24
Chapter 7: **Do Your Homework**	27
Chapter 8: **Downtime and Your Personal Well-Being**	30
Chapter 9: **Putting It All Together**	33
Conclusion	37
Crisis Management Daily Worksheet: 90-Day Plan	39
Managing the Crisis – Weekly Plan Review	220

ABOUT THE AUTHOR

Eric Jackier is a professionally trained and certified speaker, trainer, and coach who teaches leadership and mentoring at the highest level by studying the great leaders of history, business, and sports—past and present.

As the Chair of the Disability Mentoring Day Program of NYC for ten years, he has brought high quality leadership and mentoring to a population of people who can benefit from someone who believes in their capabilities.

As a person who has cerebral palsy and has had to find his own way to step outside of what people believe is possible for those who are disabled, Eric knows firsthand that all things are possible.

He is inspirational proof that anyone can rise and become a leader in their own right with a solid system of support through mentoring and leadership training.

www.jtdcoaching.com

Certifications

Executive Director, The John Maxwell Team
Certified Trainer, Jack Canfield
Member and Certified Coach, International Coach Federation
The Brian Tracy Speaking Academy
John R. Wooden Certified Coach, Coaching Success Curricula
Partner Affiliate & Certified Coach, MentorPathInc

INTRODUCTION

I'm sitting in my home office writing these words as I listen to the Coronavirus Task Force give its daily briefing. Like the rest of America, I'm following the state and federal guidelines that mandate I stay in my home indefinitely to avoid spreading or catching the virus. This health pandemic has done something I would have deemed impossible as little as thirty days ago—it has literally shut down the United States of America in just about every capacity you can think of.

Offices—including government offices like the DMV and Social Security—are closed. Sports have ceased to exist. Bars and restaurants are closed to the public except for take-out and delivery. Need a haircut? Forget it! Any business deemed non-essential is closed until further notice. Crowds have been banned. If you enjoy watching certain television shows, be prepared to have them interrupted by briefings from your governor or public health officials. The court system has been shut down except for the most urgent criminal cases, and just about every school system and university has been closed. I went to the supermarket this week, and as I was returning home, I drove down a street that's normally very busy during the day—I suddenly realized I was the only car on the road. Millions of people have either temporarily or permanently lost their jobs, and the booming economy has contracted about twenty percent.

And we aren't done yet.

As I read what I just wrote, it seems like a terrible nightmare, and yet it's real. Every single American has been affected in some way by this crisis. The federal government has passed several bills that will hopefully provide financial relief to the millions of small and medium-sized businesses that have been forced to close. Even with that relief effort, no one knows exactly how long this will go on or how long it *can* go on. No country can just shut itself down indefinitely.

This is a crisis beyond anything anyone could have ever predicted. As much as our federal, state, and local officials are doing, it will not be enough to help our local businesses survive; that task falls on each of us who own and lead our companies.

The bottom line is this: If we are to survive and prosper beyond this crisis (and we will), we *MUST* dust ourselves off and begin preparing ourselves and our businesses for what happens when the pandemic ends.

The good news is that it *can* be done; every crisis provides new opportunities for growth. There are critical steps for leaders to follow during any major crisis, and if we do, I'm optimistic we'll come back from this pandemic successfully. The time to prepare for that success is now.

As with each of my previous workbooks, I will include pertinent questions and additional information as needed. With the right leadership, we can all come through this crisis successfully. Let's get on the road to recovery!

CHAPTER ONE

Decide You Will Succeed No Matter What!

Times are hard right now, and the worst part of this crisis is the uncertainty. It won't be an easy road to recovery. Therefore, it's imperative to have a clear and focused mindset before you do anything else. As the leader, you have a responsibility to yourself, your employees, your clients and customers, and those who are depending on you to help pull them through the crisis. This will require every bit of energy and commitment you can muster.

The very first step you must take is making the decision that you will pull your company and everyone who depends on it through the crisis successfully. This must be done before anything else happens. Remember, if you make the decision that your company will survive the immediate crisis and become successful once it's over, you will have taken a key step toward making good things happen.

EXERCISE:

Write the following down:

Statement of Success

"I will do everything possible to guide my company through this crisis. I will do everything I can to find solutions to problems that arise. I will exhaust every resource legally and ethically available to me to ensure my company remains solvent and viable. I will look after the people who loyally work to carry the company mission forward each and every day. My company will weather this storm and become more successful than ever."

Put the statement somewhere you can see it every morning and evening. It will inspire you at your lowest points, and you will feel a tremendous amount of pride when you as the leader successfully steer your ship to success.

Preparing and training your mind for the job ahead and believing you will be successful are key psychological components that will dramatically increase your odds of success.

Congratulations on taking this vital first step! You are on your way to real success!

CHAPTER TWO

Develop Your Leadership Routine

We are in the middle of a worldwide health crisis with an invisible enemy. That fundamentally changes every business equation except one—crisis or no crisis, you are still the leader of your business. That fact gives you special responsibilities above and beyond what most people are dealing with right now. Part of this responsibility is keeping healthy and well, and the other part is developing your leadership routine.

I work from home under normal circumstances, so I'm pretty good at this. For others, it might take getting used to, and it certainly takes discipline. You must apply a disciplined mindset to get yourself and your company through the crisis. Here are some suggestions that have served me well over time:

1. Wake up at the usual time every day. It's the first step toward maintaining a sense of normalcy.

2. Budget your time. I like to go out in the morning, have my coffee, run whatever errands I'm able to, and prepare for my day ahead. Once I'm home, I return any calls that are urgent and go over my calendar (which is prepared a week in advance.) My coaching calls are usually sprinkled around time for reading and writing or my weekly standing conference calls with my vendors. I typically work from noon to 8 p.m. with a dinner break at 6 p.m. There are days when I might add an evening call or coaching session as late as 10 p.m. for my West Coast clients. I then stop, go over the next day's calendar, and relax before bed—12:45 a.m. sharp! This routine works for me, and whatever routine works for you is fine. Just make sure you stick to it.

3. Manage your schedule. Even if you normally delegate this to someone else, don't do it now. Setting your own schedule will help keep you engaged on a daily basis.

4. Create a private workspace. This one is crucial, especially if you're in a crowded house or apartment. You must have a place to work without being distracted or disturbed. You also need to make sure no one is allowed within that space as long as you continue or choose to work from home. Treat that area as you would if it were your office.

5. Eliminate outside distractions, just as you would if things were normal. When you're at work, you must be productive. It may help if you set aside certain hours of the day to accomplish your daily goals. You must make it clear to those around you that work time is work time and you cannot be disturbed with outside tasks.

EXERCISE:

Use the space below to do the following:

1. Create your daily schedule.

2. Figure out where you can designate your private workspace.

3. Set aside time each day for you to get your work done.

4. Put the new work schedule in the same place as your Statement of Success from the previous chapter.

CHAPTER THREE
Creating Your 90-Day Plan

Now, the real work begins! It's time to begin planning the recovery and success process. The planning should cover ninety days, which is the equivalent of a business quarter. What makes this difficult is that the plan is based on very fluid assumptions due to the constantly changing situation. What is fact today may not be fact tomorrow.

What I'm about to say may seem counterintuitive to normal business planning. The normal ninety-day plan should be written as always—with the end game as the result. The difference here is the plan should be a living document to be reviewed daily. Each day, the following questions should be asked:

- How long can I stay afloat given the current situation?
- What can I offer the public right now (if you are allowed to be open)?
- How much cash is available to me?
- Who among my employees is critical to my company's success right now?

- What critical services do I need to provide once the immediate crisis is over?
- Where can I cut costs?

Below are some questions that are less immediate but must have clear answers as the ninety-day plan takes shape:

- Is my company eligible for government assistance?
- How should I handle my creditors?
- What should I tell my clients and customers?
- How much money will I realistically make over the next ninety days? (Be *very* honest about this.)
- What are my best- and worst-case scenarios over this period?

A tip from your coach: As you begin writing your plan, be very conservative in your estimates. As an example, in my own planning, while I do think I will have some income and new opportunities, I'm planning based on *zero*. Zero-based planning is the safest way to plan during a crisis—especially when, as in this case, everything is so unpredictable. It's a lot safer to plan using the worst-case scenario. It's also less taxing mentally and emotionally if you aren't disappointed should the worst-case become reality.

CHAPTER FOUR

Communicate Often and Effectively

There is so much uncertainty in the world right now, as well as a great deal of fear and panic. One of the most important things you as a leader must do at a time like this is communicate clearly and directly with the people who depend on you for their employment and financial security.

Communication isn't always easy for a leader. I, for one, am a leader who hates giving unpleasant news. Sometimes, we have no choice. At a time like this, we as leaders must step out of our own comfort zones. Below are some suggestions as to how leaders should communicate during times of crisis:

1. **Be honest**. This is extremely important. In such uncertain times, where so much is out of our control, we must let people know what's really going on. If someone is in danger of having their hours cut or losing their job, they must know ASAP so they can prepare themselves and their families for what may

come. Be equally honest with good news. Mindset can go a long way in helping manage a crisis.

2. **Be kind.** Understanding the plight people are living through helps a great deal. Be sensitive to that plight and be as compassionate as possible when communicating.

3. **Disseminate important information.** Leaders should go out of their way to make their people feel like they're all in this together. Leaders should emphasize this repeatedly by sharing important information regarding the well-being of the business. While I'm not suggesting sharing specific financial information, I am suggesting sharing where the company stands, how it's being affected, and what measures are being taken to keep things stabilized.

4. **Communicate regularly.** Our state representatives and the Coronavirus Task Force have done an excellent job of disseminating important information on a daily basis. This has kept people informed and has also shown them how they can contribute to ending the crisis by practicing individual behaviors. That kind of communication is also helpful in business. Even if it's a simple fifteen-minute conference call at the same time every day, the more people know, the more likely they will be willing to help the leader keep things moving in the right direction. Remember, the leader cannot and *must not* do everything alone—let your team help you.

5. **The leader is human.** It isn't a sign of weakness to admit if you've made a mistake or if you're unsure of something. The idea that a leader is all-knowing and should never admit a mistake is ridiculous and, frankly, stupid. If a

mistake is made, fix it, apologize, and move forward. I promise, your people will not lose respect for you—they'll gain it.

EXERCISE:

- Make a list of who you need to communicate with on a daily and weekly basis.

- Set up a regular time each day or week as needed to share pertinent information with your employees. Do the same with key clients as necessary.

CHAPTER FIVE

Building Your Crisis Management Team

This chapter discusses one of the most critical pieces needed for success. Every leader should have a group or team of trusted advisors who bring various areas of expertise and experience to the table during a crisis. There is no leader in the world who excels in every single area of leadership. There is also no leader in the world who is immune to extreme stress and anxiety under normal circumstances, let alone a worldwide shutdown with no expiration date.

This was an area I sorely lacked in my previous company. Thus, when a crisis hit, I was completely ill-prepared, and everything I did turned out to be the wrong decision. One of the most important things I needed at that time was advice from people who knew a lot more than I did.

That occurred during "normal" times. For such uncertain and volatile times, you need advisors around you who have no agenda other than helping you as the leader manage the crisis successfully.

Below are some suggestions I have for team building based on my own experience with success and failure in crisis situations:

1. Work with a coach. This isn't as self-serving as it sounds. Working with someone outside your team who is more experienced and familiar with the issues and potential pitfalls that can occur during a crisis can be invaluable. It has made all the difference for me.

2. You will need an excellent accountant. The old saying goes, "A good leader knows the numbers." This is especially true during a crisis. I'll add something to that saying. During a crisis, especially an open-ended one, a good leader must know the numbers every day. Having a good accountant who you can trust to watch finances, and even manage them if necessary, will go a long way toward keeping the business financially secure.

3. You need a "COO." Ideally, this is someone you work closely with now or have done so in the past. Even more ideally, this person has a skill set that acts as a complement to yours. If that's the case, you are way ahead and can delegate a lot of the tasks that are better suited to that person than you. This will allow you to focus your time and energy on the most important areas that demand your immediate attention. This is equally true during normal business circumstances, but in a crisis, it's *mandatory*.

4. Mentoring can be a vital tool. It never hurts to have access to a person or people who are senior to you in experience and have managed crisis situations before. They don't necessarily have to be part of your company. Mentors can provide great insight, ideas, and solutions. Take advantage of this resource if you can!

5. Lean on family and friends. Your support system will be vital to your well-being. Contrary to what some people believe, a leader is also a human being who needs help, support, and advice. A loving and supportive family goes a long way toward keeping any leader physically, mentally, and emotionally healthy during a crisis.

EXERCISE:

Build your team! Using the space below, write down the ideal members of your crisis management team.

NAME   **RELATIONSHIP**   **KEY ROLE**

CHAPTER SIX
Talk to Your Creditors

This part is not easy and can be uncomfortable—asking for help is never easy. It's my own greatest shortcoming as a leader. That said, in times of crisis, a leader must use every tool he or she has to keep the business afloat. Here are some important things to remember when dealing with a creditor in times of crisis:

1. Be one hundred percent honest. The government has put protections in place for small businesses. However, it remains critical that you are honest and straightforward with your creditors. Tell them what you will be able to do and what you won't.

2. Honor your agreements. Do what you promise to do. If you deliver, your creditors are nearly obligated to work with you during the crisis.

3. Work together. You must understand your creditors have financial obligations to meet as well. You are part of their financial support system. If you agree to pay them on the fifteenth, do so. If you show you are a person of your word, it will go a long way, both during this crisis and in the future.

4. Communicate early and often. This is especially true if you run into a problem. Don't wait for the day before the due date to deliver bad news. If you can't make a payment, alert your creditors well ahead of time.

5. Something is better than nothing. If you see you can't make a full payment, make arrangements to make a partial payment. Anything helps. It also shows the creditor that you are making a genuine effort to make payments and meet your obligations.

EXERCISE:

1. Make a list of your creditors.

2. Determine to the best of your ability what you will be able to pay out for the next ninety days.

3. Base those computations on the idea that there will be no income. This is known as zero-based budgeting. If you know you have income, you're way ahead.

4. Create a schedule to communicate with your creditors as needed. Keep them appraised of your financial situation.

CHAPTER SEVEN
Do Your Homework

Here's a good question any leader should ask: How can I effectively use all the unexpected downtime I suddenly have to improve my business when it reopens?

If the answer doesn't come to you right away, don't worry. You now have the time to do some homework. Here are some suggestions I've used or am using to engage prospective clients, keep current within my profession, and look for new business opportunities:

1. Talk to your clients. Call, write, email—it doesn't matter. Engage with them. When doing so, it's a very good time to ask what you can do to help them through the crisis. Or perhaps ask their opinion on a new product or service you might offer. Maybe there's something you never thought of that they might suggest to help YOU through the crisis. Remember, even in times of crisis, it always pays to network.

2. Do constructive social networking. Everyone is online anyway, so why not take advantage of the circumstances? As an example, during the current situation, JTD Coaching has launched a LinkedIn campaign geared toward connecting with ideal group coaching clients. I actually did a coaching session with a business owner who was unable to return home to New York due to the international lockdown. I wonder if I'm the only coach who did an online session with someone stuck in Oman! I also connected with a US Navy chaplain. Try and use the downtime to explore new opportunities and make new connections. Even during hard times, opportunities exist—the smart leader will find them.

3. Further your professional education. This has become a staple for me since I began JTD Coaching. I've been fortunate to be trained and mentored by some of the great experts in the world on leadership and success—Brian Tracy, Jack Canfield, John Wooden, Dr. David Krueger and many others. This has given me a very solid coaching and leadership background and many interesting and effective coaching tools I use to help leaders become the best they can be. I'm always looking to improve as a coach and leader. If you're a leader, you owe it to yourself, your employees, clients, and the profession itself to be the best you possibly can. This horrible crisis provides an excellent opportunity for increased professional excellence. It can only improve your business and bottom line.

One of my new educational ventures has given me the opportunity to add a service I'm very excited about. I used to be a professional broadcaster, but I haven't done any type of broadcast in years. Through an opportunity recently presented to me, I'm learning how to deliver a professional-grade podcast. It's a tool I've wanted to explore for a long time, and I'm now investing some of my extra time into creating the Ultimate Leadership Podcast. We'll be coming to a screen near you very soon. The discussion topic will (naturally) be leadership and mentoring.

I'll keep you posted—stay tuned!

EXERCISE:

1. Contact three of your best customers and ask what you can do to help them get through the crisis. Offer your help. Seek suggestions as to how you can best serve them moving forward as we begin to reopen the economy.

2. List three ways you can use the extra time you have to create new business opportunities and relationships.

3. Look for one or two areas where you might improve your professional education.

CHAPTER EIGHT
Downtime and Your Personal Well-Being

A crisis is a crisis—they come and go. As we've discussed in earlier chapters, when a crisis hits, especially an open-ended one, the leader must step up and be at his or her best. What I'm about to say may seem counterintuitive, but it's vital to navigating through a crisis successfully: The leader *must* take downtime and make sure they're taking physical and emotional care of themselves. Daily!

We've discussed in the previous chapter what a leader can and should do for the team when possible. My question to my fellow leaders is… how are you taking care of yourself?

This particular crisis we're living through is unlike any other in our lifetime. Not just financially, but emotionally, too. There are illness and death, as well as isolation. Long-term isolation is very difficult. In my own case, the adjustment hasn't been as bad as it could have been due to the fact that I work from home anyway. I took an extra bedroom in my home and turned it into my office in order to avoid the challenges of moving around in winter weather with my physical disability. I've had very few days where I've been affected until now. My morning and evening routines have been completely altered. I regularly frequent certain restaurants, and with one exception, they're too far away to drive to during this crisis just for take-out. I haven't personally seen my closest friends in a very long time. It's very difficult and takes fortitude.

So, as a leader, how am I coping? The short answer is, I'm doing the best I can. Here are some of my own personal tips on taking care of yourself; I suggest you try some of them!

1. Change the scenery. Take a short walk, or take a drive. I make sure I change the scenery every day, and sometimes twice if I feel I'm losing it. You can do this and still practice social distancing. Do so as needed.

2. Get your rest. This is a staple of good health anyway, but in emotionally stressful times, it's vital. A leader is ineffective and no good to their company or team if they're not functioning at a high level. If I see I'm getting tired or run-down, I'll stop working, and even if it's during the day, I might take a fifteen-minute nap. If I need a day off, I'll take one. If I need to sleep for an extra hour, I'll do that. I'll do whatever I must to make sure I maintain effectiveness and not burn out.

3. Do an online chat. My family did this recently. The call included my immediate family, aunts, uncle, and cousins. I've also done video chats with several friends. It doesn't replace the physical and emotional joy and attachment that being in person brings, but it does help. Technology is an *amazing* thing.

4. Reach out. I've made a concentrated effort to get back in touch with people I haven't seen or heard from in a long time. It's a very good way to lift your spirits, and it's fun, too.

5. Read nonbusiness-related books. I'm filling the void left by a lack of baseball by reading a new book on the Top 50 New York Yankees contributors of all time (it's excellent!), as well as a very interesting book about the end of George Washington's life. It adds balance, changes the subject away from the crisis, and helps clear the mind.

CHAPTER NINE
Putting It All Together

This chapter is designed to prepare you for the final two exercises, which contain the tools I'm giving you to construct your ninety-day plan. I wish I could give you individual help as you write your plan, but since I'm not able to do that directly, I want to invite you to go to the JTD Coaching website, www.jtdcoaching.com. Send me a copy of your plan, and I'll be glad to take a look for you!

As you write your plan, please understand this kind of business planning is very different from a normal quarterly plan. This plan is designed for crisis management. Therefore, there are certain important techniques that can be the difference between success and failure. Here's my prescription for a successful crisis management plan:

1. Work backward. This may seem counterintuitive, especially since normal business planning requires a leader to look forward. In a crisis situation, you

need to visualize the outcome you want to achieve before you do anything else.

2. Divide by three. Take the overall outcome you want as the end result and break it down into monthly goals. Think about what can be accomplished based on the current circumstances within the next thirty days.

3. Script your month. Use a monthly calendar for this. Prepare your month using the ideal scenario for crisis recovery. Once it's done, go over it with your crisis management team. As we discussed earlier, it's important to get their input. Once that's finished, hang it up in a place where you can see it every day. Refer to it as needed.

4. Weekly breakdown. At the end of this workbook, you'll find several weekly worksheets. Follow my lead here and fill these out—except, of course, the bottom columns, which should be reviewed at the end of each week.

5. Ground level. As I'm sure you've figured out, what I'm trying to show you is how to manage the crisis on a granular level. Working backward allows the leader to focus on the business at its roots. Think of the business as a tree. If the roots are strong and healthy, the business—much like a tree—will prosper. The leader must ensure that happens. The root of the business occurs each and every day. By scripting your day and organizing it very specifically, you will be way ahead of the curve.

What Is Scripting?

I learned the technique of scripting from Bill Walsh, the legendary football coach of the San Francisco 49ers. In one of his many books, he shared how he "scripted" the first fifteen plays of every game based on the strengths and weaknesses of the team's opponent that week. He believed it gave him a distinct advantage, in that he would usually score first and immediately put the other team at a disadvantage mentally. The results Coach Walsh achieved speak for themselves.

Follow the Script… Until You Can't

The trouble with managing a disaster is its unpredictable nature. Our current national crisis illustrates that perfectly. Use the script you write, but be prepared for anything.

Important Tips for Building the Crisis Plan

- Be flexible at all times, as the conditions during the crisis can change at any point.

- Keep it simple.

- Focus on what the business does well. Figure out how it can deliver results immediately.

- Remove those products and services that have little or no value.

- Make sure you have enough money in the bank to cover the ninety days of the plan.

- Use zero-based budgeting (based on the idea that there will be no revenue for ninety days).

- Build the plan with your best customers in mind.

- Identify what your key revenue streams will be. How quickly can you get them up and running?

- Identify your *key* people and put them to work in executing the plan.

- Make sure you have all the key information. Make adjustments as necessary.

- Do a daily review, then do a weekly review.

- Be prepared for anything.

Crisis management is a lot to handle for any leader. The important thing is to keep calm and lead with strength, courage, and confidence. Remember, everyone is watching!

Action Steps

1. Go through the next two exercises and familiarize yourself with the daily worksheets, then the weekly worksheets.

2. Build your ninety-day crisis recovery plan.

3. **Be successful**! More so now than ever!

CONCLUSION

I truly wish I could wave a wand and tell everyone that everything will be okay and we will all come back stronger and better than ever. I happen to believe that will be the case. But I can't say I know it for sure. Nobody can.

As I sit in my home, surrounded by the deafening silence, all I can think of is the resilience of the American spirit and how we as a country have overcome amazing and incredible odds throughout our history. The American Revolution itself was as improbable an occurrence as anything you can think of. We won against all odds and built the greatest country in the history of the world.

I have no doubt we *will* survive the crisis and come out of it more successful than ever. The way this will happen is through successful leadership. Not just the political kind—the kind where all of us who are leaders decide that despite the horrible and tragic circumstances we're currently facing, we will survive and thrive.

As I write these words, it seems that from a medical perspective, we may be seeing a faint light at the end of the tunnel. What that means is the time for mourning and self-pity is over. It's time for all of us to plan for our collective comeback. That's our job as leaders, and we're all responsible for doing our part to expedite our individual and collective recovery.

I wrote this workbook based on what I've learned about leadership and crisis management. For better or worse, I've had a lot of experience with both. I take my responsibility as a business leader and professional coach very seriously. I hope this workbook helps. Our journey to recovery will be long and hard but, ultimately, successful.

I wish you good luck. Please be in touch if I can help.

We can do it!

Crisis Management Daily Worksheet: 90-Day Plan

Crisis Management Daily Worksheet: 90-Day Plan
Day 1

Daily tasks:

1.

2.

3.

4.

5.

Daily communications:

1.

2.

3.

4.

5.

What went well today?

What went wrong?

How am I feeling today as the leader of my business?

What can I do tomorrow better than I did today to keep things moving forward?

Eric Jackier

Crisis Management Daily Worksheet: 90-Day Plan
Day 2

Daily tasks:

1.

2.

3.

4.

5.

Daily communications:

1.

2.

3.

4.

5.

What went well today?

What went wrong?

How am I feeling today as the leader of my business?

What can I do tomorrow better than I did today to keep things moving forward?

Crisis Management Daily Worksheet: 90-Day Plan

Day 3

Daily tasks:

1.

2.

3.

4.

5.

Daily communications:

1.

2.

3.

4.

5.

What went well today?

What went wrong?

How am I feeling today as the leader of my business?

What can I do tomorrow better than I did today to keep things moving forward?

Eric Jackier

Crisis Management Daily Worksheet: 90-Day Plan
Day 4

Daily tasks:

1.

2.

3.

4.

5.

Daily communications:

1.

2.

3.

4.

5.

What went well today?

The Ultimate Leadership Workbook for Crisis Management

What went wrong?

How am I feeling today as the leader of my business?

What can I do tomorrow better than I did today to keep things moving forward?

Crisis Management Daily Worksheet: 90-Day Plan
Day 5

Daily tasks:

1.

2.

3.

4.

5.

Daily communications:

1.

2.

3.

4.

5.

What went well today?

The Ultimate Leadership Workbook for Crisis Management

What went wrong?

How am I feeling today as the leader of my business?

What can I do tomorrow better than I did today to keep things moving forward?

Crisis Management Daily Worksheet: 90-Day Plan

Day 6

Daily tasks:

1.

2.

3.

4.

5.

Daily communications:

1.

2.

3.

4.

5.

What went well today?

What went wrong?

How am I feeling today as the leader of my business?

What can I do tomorrow better than I did today to keep things moving forward?

Crisis Management Daily Worksheet: 90-Day Plan
Day 7

Daily tasks:

1.

2.

3.

4.

5.

Daily communications:

1.

2.

3.

4.

5.

What went well today?

What went wrong?

How am I feeling today as the leader of my business?

What can I do tomorrow better than I did today to keep things moving forward?

Crisis Management Daily Worksheet: 90-Day Plan
Day 8

Daily tasks:

1.

2.

3.

4.

5.

Daily communications:

1.

2.

3.

4.

5.

What went well today?

What went wrong?

How am I feeling today as the leader of my business?

What can I do tomorrow better than I did today to keep things moving forward?

Crisis Management Daily Worksheet: 90-Day Plan
Day 9

Daily tasks:

1.

2.

3.

4.

5.

Daily communications:

1.

2.

3.

4.

5.

What went well today?

What went wrong?

How am I feeling today as the leader of my business?

What can I do tomorrow better than I did today to keep things moving forward?

Crisis Management Daily Worksheet: 90-Day Plan
Day 10

Daily tasks:

1.

2.

3.

4.

5.

Daily communications:

1.

2.

3.

4.

5.

What went well today?

What went wrong?

How am I feeling today as the leader of my business?

What can I do tomorrow better than I did today to keep things moving forward?

Crisis Management Daily Worksheet: 90-Day Plan
Day 11

Daily tasks:

1.

2.

3.

4.

5.

Daily communications:

1.

2.

3.

4.

5.

What went well today?

What went wrong?

How am I feeling today as the leader of my business?

What can I do tomorrow better than I did today to keep things moving forward?

Crisis Management Daily Worksheet: 90-Day Plan

Day 12

Daily tasks:

1.

2.

3.

4.

5.

Daily communications:

1.

2.

3.

4.

5.

What went well today?

What went wrong?

How am I feeling today as the leader of my business?

What can I do tomorrow better than I did today to keep things moving forward?

Eric Jackier

Crisis Management Daily Worksheet: 90-Day Plan
Day 13

Daily tasks:

1.

2.

3.

4.

5.

Daily communications:

1.

2.

3.

4.

5.

What went well today?

What went wrong?

How am I feeling today as the leader of my business?

What can I do tomorrow better than I did today to keep things moving forward?

Crisis Management Daily Worksheet: 90-Day Plan
Day 14

Daily tasks:

1.

2.

3.

4.

5.

Daily communications:

1.

2.

3.

4.

5.

What went well today?

What went wrong?

How am I feeling today as the leader of my business?

What can I do tomorrow better than I did today to keep things moving forward?

Crisis Management Daily Worksheet: 90-Day Plan
Day 15

Daily tasks:

1.

2.

3.

4.

5.

Daily communications:

1.

2.

3.

4.

5.

What went well today?

What went wrong?

How am I feeling today as the leader of my business?

What can I do tomorrow better than I did today to keep things moving forward?

Crisis Management Daily Worksheet: 90-Day Plan

Day 16

Daily tasks:

1.

2.

3.

4.

5.

Daily communications:

1.

2.

3.

4.

5.

What went well today?

What went wrong?

How am I feeling today as the leader of my business?

What can I do tomorrow better than I did today to keep things moving forward?

Crisis Management Daily Worksheet: 90-Day Plan
Day 17

Daily tasks:

1.

2.

3.

4.

5.

Daily communications:

1.

2.

3.

4.

5.

What went well today?

What went wrong?

How am I feeling today as the leader of my business?

What can I do tomorrow better than I did today to keep things moving forward?

Eric Jackier

Crisis Management Daily Worksheet: 90-Day Plan

Day 18

Daily tasks:

1.

2.

3.

4.

5.

Daily communications:

1.

2.

3.

4.

5.

What went well today?

What went wrong?

How am I feeling today as the leader of my business?

What can I do tomorrow better than I did today to keep things moving forward?

Crisis Management Daily Worksheet: 90-Day Plan

Day 19

Daily tasks:

1.

2.

3.

4.

5.

Daily communications:

1.

2.

3.

4.

5.

What went well today?

What went wrong?

How am I feeling today as the leader of my business?

What can I do tomorrow better than I did today to keep things moving forward?

Eric Jackier

Crisis Management Daily Worksheet: 90-Day Plan
Day 20

Daily tasks:

1.

2.

3.

4.

5.

Daily communications:

1.

2.

3.

4.

5.

What went well today?

What went wrong?

How am I feeling today as the leader of my business?

What can I do tomorrow better than I did today to keep things moving forward?

Crisis Management Daily Worksheet: 90-Day Plan
Day 21

Daily tasks:

1.

2.

3.

4.

5.

Daily communications:

1.

2.

3.

4.

5.

What went well today?

What went wrong?

How am I feeling today as the leader of my business?

What can I do tomorrow better than I did today to keep things moving forward?

Crisis Management Daily Worksheet: 90-Day Plan
Day 22

Daily tasks:

1.

2.

3.

4.

5.

Daily communications:

1.

2.

3.

4.

5.

What went well today?

What went wrong?

How am I feeling today as the leader of my business?

What can I do tomorrow better than I did today to keep things moving forward?

Eric Jackier

Crisis Management Daily Worksheet: 90-Day Plan
Day 23

Daily tasks:

1.

2.

3.

4.

5.

Daily communications:

1.

2.

3.

4.

5.

What went well today?

What went wrong?

How am I feeling today as the leader of my business?

What can I do tomorrow better than I did today to keep things moving forward?

Crisis Management Daily Worksheet: 90-Day Plan
Day 24

Daily tasks:

1.

2.

3.

4.

5.

Daily communications:

1.

2.

3.

4.

5.

What went well today?

What went wrong?

How am I feeling today as the leader of my business?

What can I do tomorrow better than I did today to keep things moving forward?

Crisis Management Daily Worksheet: 90-Day Plan

Day 25

Daily tasks:

1.

2.

3.

4.

5.

Daily communications:

1.

2.

3.

4.

5.

What went well today?

What went wrong?

How am I feeling today as the leader of my business?

What can I do tomorrow better than I did today to keep things moving forward?

Crisis Management Daily Worksheet: 90-Day Plan

Day 26

Daily tasks:

1.

2.

3.

4.

5.

Daily communications:

1.

2.

3.

4.

5.

What went well today?

The Ultimate Leadership Workbook for Crisis Management

What went wrong?

How am I feeling today as the leader of my business?

What can I do tomorrow better than I did today to keep things moving forward?

Crisis Management Daily Worksheet: 90-Day Plan
Day 27

Daily tasks:

1.

2.

3.

4.

5.

Daily communications:

1.

2.

3.

4.

5.

What went well today?

What went wrong?

How am I feeling today as the leader of my business?

What can I do tomorrow better than I did today to keep things moving forward?

Crisis Management Daily Worksheet: 90-Day Plan
Day 28

Daily tasks:

1.

2.

3.

4.

5.

Daily communications:

1.

2.

3.

4.

5.

What went well today?

What went wrong?

How am I feeling today as the leader of my business?

What can I do tomorrow better than I did today to keep things moving forward?

Crisis Management Daily Worksheet: 90-Day Plan
Day 29

Daily tasks:

1.

2.

3.

4.

5.

Daily communications:

1.

2.

3.

4.

5.

What went well today?

What went wrong?

How am I feeling today as the leader of my business?

What can I do tomorrow better than I did today to keep things moving forward?

Crisis Management Daily Worksheet: 90-Day Plan

Day 30

Daily tasks:

1.

2.

3.

4.

5.

Daily communications:

1.

2.

3.

4.

5.

What went well today?

What went wrong?

How am I feeling today as the leader of my business?

What can I do tomorrow better than I did today to keep things moving forward?

Crisis Management Daily Worksheet: 90-Day Plan
Day 31

Daily tasks:

1.

2.

3.

4.

5.

Daily communications:

1.

2.

3.

4.

5.

What went well today?

What went wrong?

How am I feeling today as the leader of my business?

What can I do tomorrow better than I did today to keep things moving forward?

Crisis Management Daily Worksheet: 90-Day Plan
Day 32

Daily tasks:

1.

2.

3.

4.

5.

Daily communications:

1.

2.

3.

4.

5.

What went well today?

What went wrong?

How am I feeling today as the leader of my business?

What can I do tomorrow better than I did today to keep things moving forward?

Crisis Management Daily Worksheet: 90-Day Plan
Day 33

Daily tasks:

1.

2.

3.

4.

5.

Daily communications:

1.

2.

3.

4.

5.

What went well today?

What went wrong?

How am I feeling today as the leader of my business?

What can I do tomorrow better than I did today to keep things moving forward?

Crisis Management Daily Worksheet: 90-Day Plan
Day 34

Daily tasks:

1.

2.

3.

4.

5.

Daily communications:

1.

2.

3.

4.

5.

What went well today?

What went wrong?

How am I feeling today as the leader of my business?

What can I do tomorrow better than I did today to keep things moving forward?

Eric Jackier

Crisis Management Daily Worksheet: 90-Day Plan
Day 35

Daily tasks:

1.

2.

3.

4.

5.

Daily communications:

1.

2.

3.

4.

5.

What went well today?

What went wrong?

How am I feeling today as the leader of my business?

What can I do tomorrow better than I did today to keep things moving forward?

Crisis Management Daily Worksheet: 90-Day Plan
Day 36

Daily tasks:

1.

2.

3.

4.

5.

Daily communications:

1.

2.

3.

4.

5.

What went well today?

What went wrong?

How am I feeling today as the leader of my business?

What can I do tomorrow better than I did today to keep things moving forward?

Crisis Management Daily Worksheet: 90-Day Plan
Day 37

Daily tasks:

1.

2.

3.

4.

5.

Daily communications:

1.

2.

3.

4.

5.

What went well today?

What went wrong?

How am I feeling today as the leader of my business?

What can I do tomorrow better than I did today to keep things moving forward?

Crisis Management Daily Worksheet: 90-Day Plan
Day 38

Daily tasks:

1.

2.

3.

4.

5.

Daily communications:

1.

2.

3.

4.

5.

What went well today?

What went wrong?

How am I feeling today as the leader of my business?

What can I do tomorrow better than I did today to keep things moving forward?

Crisis Management Daily Worksheet: 90-Day Plan
Day 39

Daily tasks:

1.

2.

3.

4.

5.

Daily communications:

1.

2.

3.

4.

5.

What went well today?

What went wrong?

How am I feeling today as the leader of my business?

What can I do tomorrow better than I did today to keep things moving forward?

Crisis Management Daily Worksheet: 90-Day Plan

Day 40

Daily tasks:

1.

2.

3.

4.

5.

Daily communications:

1.

2.

3.

4.

5.

What went well today?

What went wrong?

How am I feeling today as the leader of my business?

What can I do tomorrow better than I did today to keep things moving forward?

Crisis Management Daily Worksheet: 90-Day Plan
Day 41

Daily tasks:

1.

2.

3.

4.

5.

Daily communications:

1.

2.

3.

4.

5.

What went well today?

What went wrong?

How am I feeling today as the leader of my business?

What can I do tomorrow better than I did today to keep things moving forward?

Crisis Management Daily Worksheet: 90-Day Plan
Day 42

Daily tasks:

1.

2.

3.

4.

5.

Daily communications:

1.

2.

3.

4.

5.

What went well today?

What went wrong?

How am I feeling today as the leader of my business?

What can I do tomorrow better than I did today to keep things moving forward?

Crisis Management Daily Worksheet: 90-Day Plan
Day 43

Daily tasks:

1.

2.

3.

4.

5.

Daily communications:

1.

2.

3.

4.

5.

What went well today?

What went wrong?

How am I feeling today as the leader of my business?

What can I do tomorrow better than I did today to keep things moving forward?

Crisis Management Daily Worksheet: 90-Day Plan
Day 44

Daily tasks:

1.

2.

3.

4.

5.

Daily communications:

1.

2.

3.

4.

5.

What went well today?

What went wrong?

How am I feeling today as the leader of my business?

What can I do tomorrow better than I did today to keep things moving forward?

Crisis Management Daily Worksheet: 90-Day Plan
Day 45

Daily tasks:

1.

2.

3.

4.

5.

Daily communications:

1.

2.

3.

4.

5.

What went well today?

What went wrong?

How am I feeling today as the leader of my business?

What can I do tomorrow better than I did today to keep things moving forward?

Eric Jackier

Crisis Management Daily Worksheet: 90-Day Plan
Day 46

Daily tasks:

1.

2.

3.

4.

5.

Daily communications:

1.

2.

3.

4.

5.

What went well today?

What went wrong?

How am I feeling today as the leader of my business?

What can I do tomorrow better than I did today to keep things moving forward?

Crisis Management Daily Worksheet: 90-Day Plan
Day 47

Daily tasks:

1.

2.

3.

4.

5.

Daily communications:

1.

2.

3.

4.

5.

What went well today?

What went wrong?

How am I feeling today as the leader of my business?

What can I do tomorrow better than I did today to keep things moving forward?

Crisis Management Daily Worksheet: 90-Day Plan
Day 48

Daily tasks:

1.

2.

3.

4.

5.

Daily communications:

1.

2.

3.

4.

5.

What went well today?

What went wrong?

How am I feeling today as the leader of my business?

What can I do tomorrow better than I did today to keep things moving forward?

Crisis Management Daily Worksheet: 90-Day Plan
Day 49

Daily tasks:

1.

2.

3.

4.

5.

Daily communications:

1.

2.

3.

4.

5.

What went well today?

What went wrong?

How am I feeling today as the leader of my business?

What can I do tomorrow better than I did today to keep things moving forward?

Crisis Management Daily Worksheet: 90-Day Plan
Day 50

Daily tasks:

1.

2.

3.

4.

5.

Daily communications:

1.

2.

3.

4.

5.

What went well today?

What went wrong?

How am I feeling today as the leader of my business?

What can I do tomorrow better than I did today to keep things moving forward?

Crisis Management Daily Worksheet: 90-Day Plan
Day 51

Daily tasks:

1.

2.

3.

4.

5.

Daily communications:

1.

2.

3.

4.

5.

What went well today?

What went wrong?

How am I feeling today as the leader of my business?

What can I do tomorrow better than I did today to keep things moving forward?

Crisis Management Daily Worksheet: 90-Day Plan
Day 52

Daily tasks:

1.

2.

3.

4.

5.

Daily communications:

1.

2.

3.

4.

5.

What went well today?

What went wrong?

How am I feeling today as the leader of my business?

What can I do tomorrow better than I did today to keep things moving forward?

Crisis Management Daily Worksheet: 90-Day Plan
Day 53

Daily tasks:

1.

2.

3.

4.

5.

Daily communications:

1.

2.

3.

4.

5.

What went well today?

What went wrong?

How am I feeling today as the leader of my business?

What can I do tomorrow better than I did today to keep things moving forward?

Eric Jackier

Crisis Management Daily Worksheet: 90-Day Plan
Day 54

Daily tasks:

1.

2.

3.

4.

5.

Daily communications:

1.

2.

3.

4.

5.

What went well today?

What went wrong?

How am I feeling today as the leader of my business?

What can I do tomorrow better than I did today to keep things moving forward?

Eric Jackier

Crisis Management Daily Worksheet: 90-Day Plan
Day 55

Daily tasks:

1.

2.

3.

4.

5.

Daily communications:

1.

2.

3.

4.

5.

What went well today?

What went wrong?

How am I feeling today as the leader of my business?

What can I do tomorrow better than I did today to keep things moving forward?

Crisis Management Daily Worksheet: 90-Day Plan
Day 56

Daily tasks:

1.

2.

3.

4.

5.

Daily communications:

1.

2.

3.

4.

5.

What went well today?

What went wrong?

How am I feeling today as the leader of my business?

What can I do tomorrow better than I did today to keep things moving forward?

Crisis Management Daily Worksheet: 90-Day Plan
Day 57

Daily tasks:

1.

2.

3.

4.

5.

Daily communications:

1.

2.

3.

4.

5.

What went well today?

What went wrong?

How am I feeling today as the leader of my business?

What can I do tomorrow better than I did today to keep things moving forward?

Eric Jackier

Crisis Management Daily Worksheet: 90-Day Plan
Day 58

Daily tasks:

1.

2.

3.

4.

5.

Daily communications:

1.

2.

3.

4.

5.

What went well today?

What went wrong?

How am I feeling today as the leader of my business?

What can I do tomorrow better than I did today to keep things moving forward?

Crisis Management Daily Worksheet: 90-Day Plan

Day 59

Daily tasks:

1.

2.

3.

4.

5.

Daily communications:

1.

2.

3.

4.

5.

What went well today?

What went wrong?

How am I feeling today as the leader of my business?

What can I do tomorrow better than I did today to keep things moving forward?

Crisis Management Daily Worksheet: 90-Day Plan

Day 60

Daily tasks:

1.

2.

3.

4.

5.

Daily communications:

1.

2.

3.

4.

5.

What went well today?

What went wrong?

How am I feeling today as the leader of my business?

What can I do tomorrow better than I did today to keep things moving forward?

Crisis Management Daily Worksheet: 90-Day Plan
Day 61

Daily tasks:

1.

2.

3.

4.

5.

Daily communications:

1.

2.

3.

4.

5.

What went well today?

What went wrong?

How am I feeling today as the leader of my business?

What can I do tomorrow better than I did today to keep things moving forward?

Crisis Management Daily Worksheet: 90-Day Plan
Day 62

Daily tasks:

1.

2.

3.

4.

5.

Daily communications:

1.

2.

3.

4.

5.

What went well today?

What went wrong?

How am I feeling today as the leader of my business?

What can I do tomorrow better than I did today to keep things moving forward?

Crisis Management Daily Worksheet: 90-Day Plan
Day 63

Daily tasks:

1.

2.

3.

4.

5.

Daily communications:

1.

2.

3.

4.

5.

What went well today?

What went wrong?

How am I feeling today as the leader of my business?

What can I do tomorrow better than I did today to keep things moving forward?

Crisis Management Daily Worksheet: 90-Day Plan
Day 64

Daily tasks:

1.

2.

3.

4.

5.

Daily communications:

1.

2.

3.

4.

5.

What went well today?

What went wrong?

How am I feeling today as the leader of my business?

What can I do tomorrow better than I did today to keep things moving forward?

Crisis Management Daily Worksheet: 90-Day Plan
Day 65

Daily tasks:

1.

2.

3.

4.

5.

Daily communications:

1.

2.

3.

4.

5.

What went well today?

What went wrong?

How am I feeling today as the leader of my business?

What can I do tomorrow better than I did today to keep things moving forward?

Crisis Management Daily Worksheet: 90-Day Plan
Day 66

Daily tasks:

1.

2.

3.

4.

5.

Daily communications:

1.

2.

3.

4.

5.

What went well today?

What went wrong?

How am I feeling today as the leader of my business?

What can I do tomorrow better than I did today to keep things moving forward?

Crisis Management Daily Worksheet: 90-Day Plan
Day 67

Daily tasks:

1.

2.

3.

4.

5.

Daily communications:

1.

2.

3.

4.

5.

What went well today?

What went wrong?

How am I feeling today as the leader of my business?

What can I do tomorrow better than I did today to keep things moving forward?

Crisis Management Daily Worksheet: 90-Day Plan
Day 68

Daily tasks:

1.

2.

3.

4.

5.

Daily communications:

1.

2.

3.

4.

5.

What went well today?

What went wrong?

How am I feeling today as the leader of my business?

What can I do tomorrow better than I did today to keep things moving forward?

Eric Jackier

Crisis Management Daily Worksheet: 90-Day Plan
Day 69

Daily tasks:

1.

2.

3.

4.

5.

Daily communications:

1.

2.

3.

4.

5.

What went well today?

What went wrong?

How am I feeling today as the leader of my business?

What can I do tomorrow better than I did today to keep things moving forward?

Crisis Management Daily Worksheet: 90-Day Plan
Day 70

Daily tasks:

1.

2.

3.

4.

5.

Daily communications:

1.

2.

3.

4.

5.

What went well today?

What went wrong?

How am I feeling today as the leader of my business?

What can I do tomorrow better than I did today to keep things moving forward?

Crisis Management Daily Worksheet: 90-Day Plan
Day 71

Daily tasks:

1.

2.

3.

4.

5.

Daily communications:

1.

2.

3.

4.

5.

What went well today?

What went wrong?

How am I feeling today as the leader of my business?

What can I do tomorrow better than I did today to keep things moving forward?

Crisis Management Daily Worksheet: 90-Day Plan
Day 72

Daily tasks:

1.

2.

3.

4.

5.

Daily communications:

1.

2.

3.

4.

5.

What went well today?

What went wrong?

How am I feeling today as the leader of my business?

What can I do tomorrow better than I did today to keep things moving forward?

Crisis Management Daily Worksheet: 90-Day Plan
Day 73

Daily tasks:

1.

2.

3.

4.

5.

Daily communications:

1.

2.

3.

4.

5.

What went well today?

What went wrong?

How am I feeling today as the leader of my business?

What can I do tomorrow better than I did today to keep things moving forward?

Crisis Management Daily Worksheet: 90-Day Plan
Day 74

Daily tasks:

1.

2.

3.

4.

5.

Daily communications:

1.

2.

3.

4.

5.

What went well today?

What went wrong?

How am I feeling today as the leader of my business?

What can I do tomorrow better than I did today to keep things moving forward?

Crisis Management Daily Worksheet: 90-Day Plan
Day 75

Daily tasks:

1.

2.

3.

4.

5.

Daily communications:

1.

2.

3.

4.

5.

What went well today?

What went wrong?

How am I feeling today as the leader of my business?

What can I do tomorrow better than I did today to keep things moving forward?

Crisis Management Daily Worksheet: 90-Day Plan
Day 76

Daily tasks:

1.

2.

3.

4.

5.

Daily communications:

1.

2.

3.

4.

5.

What went well today?

What went wrong?

How am I feeling today as the leader of my business?

What can I do tomorrow better than I did today to keep things moving forward?

Eric Jackier

Crisis Management Daily Worksheet: 90-Day Plan
Day 77

Daily tasks:

1.

2.

3.

4.

5.

Daily communications:

1.

2.

3.

4.

5.

What went well today?

What went wrong?

How am I feeling today as the leader of my business?

What can I do tomorrow better than I did today to keep things moving forward?

Crisis Management Daily Worksheet: 90-Day Plan
Day 78

Daily tasks:

1.

2.

3.

4.

5.

Daily communications:

1.

2.

3.

4.

5.

What went well today?

What went wrong?

How am I feeling today as the leader of my business?

What can I do tomorrow better than I did today to keep things moving forward?

Eric Jackier

Crisis Management Daily Worksheet: 90-Day Plan
Day 79

Daily tasks:

1.

2.

3.

4.

5.

Daily communications:

1.

2.

3.

4.

5.

What went well today?

What went wrong?

How am I feeling today as the leader of my business?

What can I do tomorrow better than I did today to keep things moving forward?

Eric Jackier

Crisis Management Daily Worksheet: 90-Day Plan
Day 80

Daily tasks:

1.

2.

3.

4.

5.

Daily communications:

1.

2.

3.

4.

5.

What went well today?

What went wrong?

How am I feeling today as the leader of my business?

What can I do tomorrow better than I did today to keep things moving forward?

Eric Jackier

Crisis Management Daily Worksheet: 90-Day Plan
Day 81

Daily tasks:

1.

2.

3.

4.

5.

Daily communications:

1.

2.

3.

4.

5.

What went well today?

What went wrong?

How am I feeling today as the leader of my business?

What can I do tomorrow better than I did today to keep things moving forward?

Crisis Management Daily Worksheet: 90-Day Plan
Day 82

Daily tasks:

1.

2.

3.

4.

5.

Daily communications:

1.

2.

3.

4.

5.

What went well today?

What went wrong?

How am I feeling today as the leader of my business?

What can I do tomorrow better than I did today to keep things moving forward?

Eric Jackier

Crisis Management Daily Worksheet: 90-Day Plan
Day 83

Daily tasks:

1.

2.

3.

4.

5.

Daily communications:

1.

2.

3.

4.

5.

What went well today?

What went wrong?

How am I feeling today as the leader of my business?

What can I do tomorrow better than I did today to keep things moving forward?

Crisis Management Daily Worksheet: 90-Day Plan
Day 84

Daily tasks:

1.

2.

3.

4.

5.

Daily communications:

1.

2.

3.

4.

5.

What went well today?

What went wrong?

How am I feeling today as the leader of my business?

What can I do tomorrow better than I did today to keep things moving forward?

Crisis Management Daily Worksheet: 90-Day Plan
Day 85

Daily tasks:

1.

2.

3.

4.

5.

Daily communications:

1.

2.

3.

4.

5.

What went well today?

What went wrong?

How am I feeling today as the leader of my business?

What can I do tomorrow better than I did today to keep things moving forward?

Eric Jackier

Crisis Management Daily Worksheet: 90-Day Plan

Day 86

Daily tasks:

1.

2.

3.

4.

5.

Daily communications:

1.

2.

3.

4.

5.

What went well today?

What went wrong?

How am I feeling today as the leader of my business?

What can I do tomorrow better than I did today to keep things moving forward?

Crisis Management Daily Worksheet: 90-Day Plan
Day 87

Daily tasks:

1.

2.

3.

4.

5.

Daily communications:

1.

2.

3.

4.

5.

What went well today?

What went wrong?

How am I feeling today as the leader of my business?

What can I do tomorrow better than I did today to keep things moving forward?

Crisis Management Daily Worksheet: 90-Day Plan
Day 88

Daily tasks:

1.

2.

3.

4.

5.

Daily communications:

1.

2.

3.

4.

5.

What went well today?

What went wrong?

How am I feeling today as the leader of my business?

What can I do tomorrow better than I did today to keep things moving forward?

Crisis Management Daily Worksheet: 90-Day Plan

Day 89

Daily tasks:

1.

2.

3.

4.

5.

Daily communications:

1.

2.

3.

4.

5.

What went well today?

What went wrong?

How am I feeling today as the leader of my business?

What can I do tomorrow better than I did today to keep things moving forward?

Crisis Management Daily Worksheet: 90-Day Plan
Day 90

Daily tasks:

1.

2.

3.

4.

5.

Daily communications:

1.

2.

3.

4.

5.

What went well today?

What went wrong?

How am I feeling today as the leader of my business?

What can I do tomorrow better than I did today to keep things moving forward?

Eric Jackier

Managing the Crisis:
Weekly Plan Review

Managing the Crisis: Weekly Plan Review

Week 1

Top five tasks this week:

1.

2.

3.

4.

5.

Who can I network with this week in order to create new opportunities in the future?

1.

2.

3.

4.

5.

Who must I communicate with this week? (Staff, creditors, vendors, etc.)

1.

2.

3.

4.

5.

What am I offering (products or services) this week that can help people get through the crisis? (Think about future clients.)

1.

2.

3.

What were the company expenses this week?

1.

2.

3.

What was the income?

The Ultimate Leadership Workbook for Crisis Management

What are some new projects I can introduce that can bring in revenue once we reopen?

1.

2.

3.

What have I done this week to steer the company through the crisis?

1.

2.

3.

What must I do next week to make progress?

1.

2.

3.

Additional notes and new ideas:

Eric Jackier

Managing the Crisis: Weekly Plan Review
Week 2

Top five tasks this week:

1.

2.

3.

4.

5.

Who can I network with this week in order to create new opportunities in the future?

1.

2.

3.

4.

5.

Who must I communicate with this week? (Staff, creditors, vendors, etc.)

1.

2.

3.

4.

5.

What am I offering (products or services) this week that can help people get through the crisis? (Think about future clients.)

1.

2.

3.

What were the company expenses this week?

1.

2.

3.

What was the income?

The Ultimate Leadership Workbook for Crisis Management

What are some new projects I can introduce that can bring in revenue once we reopen?

1.

2.

3.

What have I done this week to steer the company through the crisis?

1.

2.

3.

What must I do next week to make progress?

1.

2.

3.

Additional notes and new ideas:

Eric Jackier

Managing the Crisis: Weekly Plan Review

Week 3

Top five tasks this week:

1.

2.

3.

4.

5.

Who can I network with this week in order to create new opportunities in the future?

1.

2.

3.

4.

5.

Who must I communicate with this week? (Staff, creditors, vendors, etc.)

1.

2.

3.

4.

5.

What am I offering (products or services) this week that can help people get through the crisis? (Think about future clients.)

1.

2.

3.

What were the company expenses this week?

1.

2.

3.

What was the income?

The Ultimate Leadership Workbook for Crisis Management

What are some new projects I can introduce that can bring in revenue once we reopen?

1.

2.

3.

What have I done this week to steer the company through the crisis?

1.

2.

3.

What must I do next week to make progress?

1.

2.

3.

Additional notes and new ideas:

Eric Jackier

The Ultimate Leadership Workbook for Crisis Management

Managing the Crisis: Weekly Plan Review
Week 4

Top five tasks this week:

1.

2.

3.

4.

5.

Who can I network with this week in order to create new opportunities in the future?

1.

2.

3.

4.

5.

Who must I communicate with this week? (Staff, creditors, vendors, etc.)

1.

2.

3.

4.

5.

What am I offering (products or services) this week that can help people get through the crisis? (Think about future clients.)

1.

2.

3.

What were the company expenses this week?

1.

2.

3.

What was the income?

What are some new projects I can introduce that can bring in revenue once we reopen?

1.

2.

3.

What have I done this week to steer the company through the crisis?

1.

2.

3.

What must I do next week to make progress?

1.

2.

3.

Additional notes and new ideas:

Eric Jackier

Managing the Crisis: Weekly Plan Review
Week 5

Top five tasks this week:

1.

2.

3.

4.

5.

Who can I network with this week in order to create new opportunities in the future?

1.

2.

3.

4.

5.

Who must I communicate with this week? (Staff, creditors, vendors, etc.)

1.

2.

3.

4.

5.

What am I offering (products or services) this week that can help people get through the crisis? (Think about future clients.)

1.

2.

3.

What were the company expenses this week?

1.

2.

3.

What was the income?

What are some new projects I can introduce that can bring in revenue once we reopen?

1.

2.

3.

What have I done this week to steer the company through the crisis?

1.

2.

3.

What must I do next week to make progress?

1.

2.

3.

Additional notes and new ideas:

Eric Jackier

Managing the Crisis: Weekly Plan Review

Week 6

Top five tasks this week:

1.

2.

3.

4.

5.

Who can I network with this week in order to create new opportunities in the future?

1.

2.

3.

4.

5.

Who must I communicate with this week? (Staff, creditors, vendors, etc.)

1.

2.

3.

4.

5.

What am I offering (products or services) this week that can help people get through the crisis? (Think about future clients.)

1.

2.

3.

What were the company expenses this week?

1.

2.

3.

What was the income?

What are some new projects I can introduce that can bring in revenue once we reopen?

1.

2.

3.

What have I done this week to steer the company through the crisis?

1.

2.

3.

What must I do next week to make progress?

1.

2.

3.

Additional notes and new ideas:

Eric Jackier

Managing the Crisis: Weekly Plan Review
Week 7

Top five tasks this week:

1.

2.

3.

4.

5.

Who can I network with this week in order to create new opportunities in the future?

1.

2.

3.

4.

5.

Who must I communicate with this week? (Staff, creditors, vendors, etc.)

1.

2.

3.

4.

5.

What am I offering (products or services) this week that can help people get through the crisis? (Think about future clients.)

1.

2.

3.

What were the company expenses this week?

1.

2.

3.

What was the income?

What are some new projects I can introduce that can bring in revenue once we reopen?

1.

2.

3.

What have I done this week to steer the company through the crisis?

1.

2.

3.

What must I do next week to make progress?

1.

2.

3.

Additional notes and new ideas:

Eric Jackier

Managing the Crisis: Weekly Plan Review
Week 8

Top five tasks this week:

1.

2.

3.

4.

5.

Who can I network with this week in order to create new opportunities in the future?

1.

2.

3.

4.

5.

Who must I communicate with this week? (Staff, creditors, vendors, etc.)

1.

2.

3.

4.

5.

What am I offering (products or services) this week that can help people get through the crisis? (Think about future clients.)

1.

2.

3.

What were the company expenses this week?

1.

2.

3.

What was the income?

What are some new projects I can introduce that can bring in revenue once we reopen?

1.

2.

3.

What have I done this week to steer the company through the crisis?

1.

2.

3.

What must I do next week to make progress?

1.

2.

3.

Additional notes and new ideas:

Eric Jackier

The Ultimate Leadership Workbook for Crisis Management

Managing the Crisis: Weekly Plan Review
Week 9

Top five tasks this week:

1.

2.

3.

4.

5.

Who can I network with this week in order to create new opportunities in the future?

1.

2.

3.

4.

5.

Who must I communicate with this week? (Staff, creditors, vendors, etc.)

1.

2.

3.

4.

5.

What am I offering (products or services) this week that can help people get through the crisis? (Think about future clients.)

1.

2.

3.

What were the company expenses this week?

1.

2.

3.

What was the income?

What are some new projects I can introduce that can bring in revenue once we reopen?

1.

2.

3.

What have I done this week to steer the company through the crisis?

1.

2.

3.

What must I do next week to make progress?

1.

2.

3.

Additional notes and new ideas:

Eric Jackier

Managing the Crisis: Weekly Plan Review

Week 10

Top five tasks this week:

1.

2.

3.

4.

5.

Who can I network with this week in order to create new opportunities in the future?

1.

2.

3.

4.

5.

Who must I communicate with this week? (Staff, creditors, vendors, etc.)

1.

2.

3.

4.

5.

What am I offering (products or services) this week that can help people get through the crisis? (Think about future clients.)

1.

2.

3.

What were the company expenses this week?

1.

2.

3.

What was the income?

What are some new projects I can introduce that can bring in revenue once we reopen?

1.

2.

3.

What have I done this week to steer the company through the crisis?

1.

2.

3.

What must I do next week to make progress?

1.

2.

3.

Additional notes and new ideas:

Eric Jackier

Managing the Crisis: Weekly Plan Review
Week 11

Top five tasks this week:

1.

2.

3.

4.

5.

Who can I network with this week in order to create new opportunities in the future?

1.

2.

3.

4.

5.

Who must I communicate with this week? (Staff, creditors, vendors, etc.)

1.

2.

3.

4.

5.

What am I offering (products or services) this week that can help people get through the crisis? (Think about future clients.)

1.

2.

3.

What were the company expenses this week?

1.

2.

3.

What was the income?

What are some new projects I can introduce that can bring in revenue once we reopen?

1.

2.

3.

What have I done this week to steer the company through the crisis?

1.

2.

3.

What must I do next week to make progress?

1.

2.

3.

Additional notes and new ideas:

Eric Jackier

Managing the Crisis: Weekly Plan Review
Week 12

Top five tasks this week:

1.

2.

3.

4.

5.

Who can I network with this week in order to create new opportunities in the future?

1.

2.

3.

4.

5.

Who must I communicate with this week? (Staff, creditors, vendors, etc.)

1.

2.

3.

4.

5.

What am I offering (products or services) this week that can help people get through the crisis? (Think about future clients.)

1.

2.

3.

What were the company expenses this week?

1.

2.

3.

What was the income?

The Ultimate Leadership Workbook for Crisis Management

What are some new projects I can introduce that can bring in revenue once we reopen?

1.

2.

3.

What have I done this week to steer the company through the crisis?

1.

2.

3.

What must I do next week to make progress?

1.

2.

3.

Additional notes and new ideas:

Eric Jackier

Copyright © 2020 by Eric Jackier

All Rights Reserved

www.ingramcontent.com/pod-product-compliance
Lightning Source LLC
Chambersburg PA
CBHW082016230526
45466CB00022B/2266